Copyright © Elizabeth Blade 2017

All rights reserved. No parts of this publication may be reproduced or transmitted in any form or by any means, electronic or mechanical, including photocopying, recording, storage in an information retrieval system, or otherwise, without the prior permission of the author.

This is a work of poetry. Any poem you read here with any resemblance of actual people, living or deceased, is purely coincidental.

For more information, go to: www.elizabethblade.com

Follow Elizabeth on Twitter: https://twitter.com/Moondance_81 (@Moondance_81)

Cover by: Amber Lynn

Also by Elizabeth Blade: *In Motion with Devotion – Volume One*

ISBN: 978-0-648-00261-1

White Light Publishing House
6 Lincoln Way
Melton West, VIC, Australia 3337

www.whitelightpublishingau.com

A Rising Moon on Domestic Violence

Elizabeth Blade

∞ Dedication ∞

This book is dedicated to you.

To the survivors of the silent ones gone before us;

we are YOUR voice.

Contents

Cannot Undo	3
Wondering When, Wondering Why	11
Tell Me Mummy – Part One	17
Tell Me Mummy – Part Two	23
You Were with Me	27
To You	35
I Sit Here	45
I Need You	57
It Needs to End	61

Acknowledgments

First of all, I would like to acknowledge my parents Betty and Eric, without your love and support this would not be possible.

Mum, I know you are shining down from me in heaven every day. I love you and miss you so very much.

To my father, Eric, who has suffered so much over the past couple of years, you have been a rock for me and I will always admire your strength and courage. Thank you for being the father that you are.

To my grandparents, Vincent and Jean, how I miss you both terribly. I will always miss you and I think of you every day. To my dearest Grandpa Vincent, thank you so much for the encouragement you have given me when it came to my dreams and my writing. You'll always be in my heart Nanna and Grandpa.

To my brother, Tom, thank you for the endless supplies of cup of teas and for listening to the words I write. (Nice going Frank) *Ha-Ha*

To my in-laws, Barry and Sue, I thank you so much for being so supportive, your kindness and love is so welcoming and I thank you both for your support.

To Deb, thank you for always being a positive word in my ear. I will never forget your encouragement and your support.

To my wonderful husband, Cobra, words cannot describe the way you make me feel. I am so lucky to have found a love like yours. Your support and edging me on to never give up will always be in my heart. Thank you so much. I love you.

To my wonderful and dear friend Maree Cutler-Naroba you have changed my life around for the better. I cannot thank you enough. Your kindness, mentorship and support has gone such a long way. I will never forget everything you have done for me. This book is in the making because of you!

I love you my friend. A huge thank you also for writing the forward of this book.

To my dear friend, Fiona, you have been a support of mine with my writing for a lot of years. You have always encouraged me and I will always remember that. I think I owe you a lunch. Thank you so much for being my friend. You have been my friend for a lot of years. Thank you for all that you do and for all that you've done. You'll always be a dear friend of mine.

Patti, thank you so much for the support you have shown me. I really appreciate the kind words and your faith in me. I really hope to make it to America someday. Lots of love and best wishes to you.

To Lanny Poffo, thank you for being such an inspiration, and thank you for always being the kind word in my ear.

Mick Foley, I love you dearly. Thank you for your undying support. Your friendship and kindness I will never ever forget.

Ronn Moss, thank you for sharing my work. That in itself, means so much. If my work never got shared to anyone, they would be words on a page that only I see. Thank you for sharing it with your world of friends, fans and followers.

To Lou Diamond Phillips, thank you! You have shared my work to the masses, I hope somewhere, someway it makes a difference in someone's life. You have definitely made a difference in mine, and I hope to meet you someday.

To everyone that has supported me over the years, **thank you!** I want to put so many names in, but that in itself would be an entire book.

Foreword

Dear Reader,

It is with pleasure that I write the foreword to this beautiful poetry book by Elizabeth Blade, a gifted poet.

The effect of a moon is to bring light into darkness. A moonlit night chases away the darkness. No longer can **domestic violence be hidden in the darkness.**

We all must take responsibility and be relentless in our pursuit to cast back the harrowing effects it has on women and children.

It is time for *A Rising Moon* on **domestic violence**.

For those who are still experiencing domestic violence, for those who are survivors of domestic violence, and for those who choose to be the voice of advocacy to reduce domestic violence, allow these poignant and soul-wrenching words to touch you at your core and evoke a response to action.

Thank you, Elizabeth, for being a domestic violence advocate. Through your powerful poetry, you encourage us to be a 'Rising Moon' – casting moonlight that breaks down the dark silence of domestic violence.

Maree Cutler-Naroba
Child Protection Researcher, Trainer and Speaker
www.childprotectiondownunder.com.au

A Message from Lanny

I have a dear friend from down under
Her name is Elizabeth Blade
She wrote a magnificent book to bring solace
To those who are so much afraid

There are too many victims of violent crime
Elizabeth Blade holds the key
Her beautiful book is a beacon of hope
If we want to be happy and free

www.geniuslannypoffo.com

About the Author

Born in Melbourne, and raised in Adelaide, Elizabeth Blade has been one thing all of her life, and that has been a dreamer. As a child, she dreamed she would someday share her words with the world. She has always imagined that her books, which forever clicked over in her mind, would be shown to all the people of the world.

Elizabeth is in the middle of writing a variety of novels and books for all ages. She also likes to write lyrics for songs and hopes that someday she can write lyrics for some of the best artists in the world.

"It is a pipe dream, but sometimes it is good to dream big".

Elizabeth also enjoys writing poetry and has been doing so since she was just a child. Writing from the tender age of just five years, she would say the words out loud as her mother would overhear and write them down. Wise beyond her years, she was destined to write what she felt and share it in abundance. **Elizabeth's goal in life is to *inspire others.*** Over the years, her poetry has helped her overcome some troubling times in her life.

Elizabeth has compiled two poetry eBooks and she is planning on working on more. Her first release, which debuted in April of 2015, was a book called *In Motion with Devotion - Volume One*. More are to follow as each volume will be something new and a change of pace in various topics.

Elizabeth wrote this book, *A Rising Moon on Domestic Violence*, through experiences witnessed or feelings that have delved inside due to media attention and news stories that are so prominent right now. A strong advocate who wants to see an end to this mindless violence, she is determined to have her voice heard. Domestic violence is in every corner of the globe, and needs to end.

Allow Elizabeth to whisk you into the world of poetry that she likes to call unique and 'a world of its own.'

"With my poetry, I want to take people on the journey with me. I want to connect with people through powerful and impacting words." - Elizabeth Blade

Find Elizabeth online:

Website: www.elizabethblade.com
Email: moondance_81@me.com
Twitter: https://twitter.com/Moondance_81 (@Moondance_81)
Facebook: www.facebook.com/ElizabethBladeWriter

Cannot Undo

Cannot Undo

I cannot undo all the things you made me do,
All I ever wanted to do was to love you.

Everything seemed so simple,
You used to laugh at my smile, with my dimples.
You would stroke my hair and tell me you loved me.

Then you went away, in walked a different you,
You shadowed into something that made me doubt this point of view.

Why do this when I love you?

Everything was right in the world, then it turned upside down,
My smile with the dimples turned into a frown.

The man I once loved was no longer around,

You started to beat me,
everything got to me and it would eat me.
Why did you change? Was it something I have done?
You hit me once and promised it wouldn't happen again.

I forgave you and we made up like lovers after a fight,
You kissed me gently, you said everything would be alright.

But look, it happened again! This time much harder.

You punched and you slapped, you pulled at my hair,
Then walked away and just left me there.

Too scared to move, left alone with my thoughts,
What did I do to cause such a vicious onslaught?
I couldn't help wonder why you would do that to me

You came on back once again later on,
Once more played the same unoriginal song.

You said again, "Baby, I lost control," inside my mind,

On my body is where it took its toll.

Again, I forgave you, thinking you would change,
but again, my face and body you would rearrange.

Everything that was wrong in your world, you'd place the blame on me.
I heard you even slept around on me.
I questioned you about it and you hit me so hard,
I was knocked unconscious.

You left me there to die,
Inside I wish I did,
So, I wouldn't have to feel my soul cry.

You said "No more, baby, I will get help",
Later that night you hit me with your belt.

Your loving hands became a distant memory to me,
I no longer had any idea who you were to me.
I remember the night I tried to leave,

One more trick you had up your sleeve,
You hit me once more as I was getting in the car to leave.

You were stopped in your tracks when a neighbour called for help.

You got arrested and cried out, "Tell them I didn't hurt you or else!"
They put you in the cop car and took you away,
Now was my time to get away.

But where to go now?
I lived with you for so many years,
My family had all gone or moved away.

I isolated myself from the world,
I always hid my face,
I tried to avoid looking anyone in the eyes,
So they wouldn't see how beaten they were.
My life has moved on, *I am strong,*
I found a new man, one who loves me and understands.

For so long I thought he would hit me, just like you did,
But deep in my heart, I hope he doesn't do what you did,
Or I might just die some more inside.

When you hit me, I died inside,
I lost myself and my pride.
Now I hope to start anew,
I hoped never again to have to see you.

To my surprise, I hear,
You were drunk when you drove your car,
You crashed and never went far,
You died a miserable death.

Although a part of me mourned for you and the better times we had,
A part of me was happy, because you could hurt no more.
Is that so wrong?
Am I so bad?

That all I ever wanted was for you to never hurt another,
We are all just sisters and brothers.

We should all get along,
We should all learn to find and sing our happy songs.

A way of life, a way of love,
Things that death doesn't know from above.

We are who we are,
We can fight to win ourselves back,
We can choose to move on, be strong and learn to love again,

We can win again.
Stop the silence and let's end this mindless violence.

Wondering When, Wondering Why

Wondering When, Wondering Why

A sweet blind love,

Suppose it was sent from heaven up above,

Suppose it flew away, like a flying dove.

First it was here, then it was gone,

It's flown away, trying to find love another way.

You say it's love, but it is lust,

You don't even know this person,

Can you trust?

Can you confide in him with all your fears?

Have you been walking around blind all these years?

Can you tell him all of your dreams?

There is something more to this,

He's not what he seems,

He's something dark and mean.

There is no longer light in your day,

It's gone into night.

When he comes home drunk,

You know once again you're going to be struck.

Again, and again the beating goes,

Your fear for him gets even worse.

You're starting to really feel the hurt,

not only on the outside,

but inside as well.

Your eyes start to swell,

You feel your tears fall.

You wonder how you ever fell in love with this beast

You're hanging onto your last breath as he beats the life out of you

Your breathing gets harder,

You cannot even breathe.

As he hits you one last time,

You're on the floor; you won't get up,

Not even a sound, you can't get up.

His screams can be heard as the dead woman lies,

The only sounds now are his drunken cries.

He runs to the kitchen,
He grabs a knife,
He plunges it into his heart,
His last breath of life and people wonder,
Why did he kill his wife?

Because this drunken beast,
he was hitting his wife,
Yet again with his fists of rage,
wishing he had turned the page.
She is dead now, this is such an outrage,
He refused to start a clean slate,
Now for both of them, it is too late.

He was killing her slowly,
at his own rate,
Because he didn't show love, only hate.
The dove did no longer fly,
It died! You can still hear the dove cry.

When will people start to wonder why?

Tell Me Mummy

Part One

Tell Me Mummy
Part One

Tell me Mummy, why did Daddy do the things he did?
Why did he hurt you and beat you?

Why did he put you down?
Why did he act so different when people were around?
He wouldn't hurt us when people were there,
That's when I liked Daddy best,
Our bruises had some time to heal.

You would stop Daddy from hurting me,
I know that you tried,
In my room alone I would cry.

I hear Mummy and Daddy yelling again,
He will hurt her some more,
I think I heard the sound of Mummy hit the floor,
Then the slam of a door,
Daddy rushes to his car and drives away.

I go to Mummy to see if she is alright,

Her eyes are closed shut and they are big and bruised,

I hate it when Daddy hurts us with his abuse.

Mummy reaches out for me, and hugs me and says, "it will be alright,"

Mummy tells me what to do, we pack some bags and run away,

On a big adventure and that's where we'll stay.

We never made it very far,

Daddy saw us walking along the side of the road and he pulled over his car,

He dragged Mummy in the car and I remember I screamed.

He drove off with Mummy and just left me there,

I remember seeing my mummy's face, she was banging on the windows screaming my name,

I screamed back for her just the same.

The lady that lived nearby heard my screaming cries and she protected me and kept me from harm,
She saw the bruises all over me and on my arm.

The police were called and I stayed with the lady, then I was taken away,
Inside I thought Mummy and I could have made it,
We could have run away.

I remember being sat down and the officer had a frown,
He told me my mummy was gone and Daddy too,
I was sitting there wondering what had happened to you.

Tell Me Mummy

Part Two

Tell Me Mummy
Part Two

Mum, I'm grown up now,

I remembered what happened that very night,

I know you tried to stay with me and you put up a fight.

I remember everything you did for me,

I remember the love you had shown,

If only you can see me now, Mum, now I'm all grown.

I am a mother now too,

I have a daughter and I have a man that I love.

He is nothing like Daddy,

He never treats me wrong,

I am finally in a place where I belong.

I don't feel fearful anymore.

I think of you all the time,

I don't think of Daddy much.

I remember the times before he changed,

The accident really hurt his way of thinking,
No longer joy would he bring.

I go to lay flowers in the river where they found you on that rainy night,
I often sit and wonder what life would have been like if you were here now.
I wish I could feel your arms around me somehow,
I wish I could see your face and tell you all that has happened in my life,
The little girl I was grew up and became a wife.

I have a little girl of my own who looks so much like you,
She is seven years old now,
The age I was when you were taken away.
But I know this, Mum, your love is never far away,
You are in my heart every single day.

I know domestic violence is wrong,
Men that treat women like that just don't belong.

You Were with Me

You Were with Me

You were with me for just a short time,
You grew in my tummy,
You were mine.

Now it's time to tell Daddy you're here,
I hope he will be pleased.
We will tell him when he comes home,
My thoughts of the future begin to roam.

What will you look like?
Are you a girl or a boy?
What will be your favourite toy?

Now it's time, my unborn child,
Daddy just pulled up in the drive,
He walks in the door.

"Hello Honey, I have some news to tell,"
He smiles and I think to myself,

"This news will go down well."

"I'm pregnant!" I say to him with glee.
Then my husband turned away from me,
"We are not ready for something like this."

"It's a fact now dear, we can do this," I say,
"We will be a Mum and a Dad,
We will be the best parents a child could have."

The man I loved turned into someone I did not know,
He screamed out the words "NO! NO! NO!"

I touched my stomach and thought to myself,
"I hope my baby couldn't hear. Daddy may not want you, but your mummy sure does."

I started to cry and he screamed again,
"GET RID OF IT!"
I looked at him with sadness and pain,
"No! It's a part of me, a part of us!"

He says, "I don't want a baby, how can you do this to me?"
I went to answer, but he hit me and he hit me hard.

He went crazy, my mind was in a daze,
He clawed, he hit, kicked and punched,
He screamed and he yelled,
Oh, dear Lord, I can feel my eyes as they swelled,
He had hit me so hard I soon passed out.

I woke up and he was gone,
I pulled myself up from the floor and walked to the bathroom,
Slowly, I looked in the mirror,
My eyes were almost swollen shut.

My body hurt all over and I was in so much pain,
My tummy hurt really bad, inside I knew he hurt you too.

I prayed to the Gods above I wasn't losing you,
A cramp doubled me over and I began to worry.

I heard him come back and I was frightened our life would end,
He screamed, "Don't you talk to me, don't even look at me!"
"You're pathetic, I don't want this kid!"
Deep inside I wish he did.

I had never seen him act this way,
How could he turn out like this?
Our marriage had always been total bliss.
How could this all go wrong in just an instant?

Suddenly the pain got worse,
I started to bleed,
I screamed, "NO! I don't want to lose you!"
My husband looked at me and he said, "It better be gone",
"That kid just does not belong."
My husband yelled, "You better clean yourself up! I am going out."

He left me there, laying on the bathroom floor,
I felt a tug in my stomach with violent cramps,

I started to cry, "What is happening to me?"

Why am I losing you?
A wave of sadness washed over me,
Please, baby, I whispered, "don't go,"
But you left me,
I lost you,
You were with me, then you were gone.
What's happening to me now?
Breathing is getting harder,
The blood is gushing out,
I can't stop the flow.
My body is going into shock.

Oh, dear God, I think I am going to die.
My baby, I lost you and I felt so very sad.
Now it looks like Mummy will be coming with you,
Daddy must have hurt both of us really bad.

The greatest love is all a mother can have,
We would have been good together,

Both mother and child.

I close my eyes and let out my last breath,
Daddy stopped loving me and you too,
Mummy lost the fight to live.
I had no choice, but to go with you.

Daddy came home and found us there,
I was gone,
I had sung my final song,
Daddy regretted what he did in a moment of madness.
All it left him with was eternal sadness.

You and I are now basked in light,
You are my love, my baby,
You were with me and now I am with you,
I love you, my angel.

To You

To You

I was looking out the window,
Looking up at the night,
Watching the twinkling of the stars,
Wishing my Mummy and Daddy
Would stop fighting and shouting.

Mummy yells and Daddy hits,
I have had enough of this,
I wonder if they'd care
If I disappeared and went away.

I start to cry quietly
And I pray for someone to take me
Away from this place,
The memories of here I want to erase.

Plates are smashing, cups get thrown,
Here I am listening and I feel so alone.

Mum and Dad, please stop this madness,
Can't we please just end the sadness?

Dad breaks down the door and screams at me,
He grabs me around the collar of my shirt and hits me.
I scream for him to let go of me.
He shouts in my ear and says,
"You're just like your mother, worthless and no good!"

He walks away and from outside I hear him yell,
"I'm leaving now, but I'll be back!"

I walk down the stairs to see my mother
Sitting at the kitchen table,
Her face is all bruised,
And broken things cover the floor,

She drinks Vodka from the bottle,
And stares at me with sadness and despair.

"Don't end up like this, please don't end up like me,

If I were you, I'd be running for all eternity."

I grabbed my mother's hand,
"Mum, you are so strong, but your mind is weak,
It's help that you now need to seek."

"Come on, let's go, let's get away,
Let's start anew, we can find a new place,
Far away from here where we will be safe."

Mother takes a big gulp from her Vodka and says,
"Beneath the beast, you see is a man that I love."
"I remember when I first met your Dad,
He was the most darling man you could ever have.
All of the time he treated me so right."

"He would buy me roses and presents out of the blue. He would always say the words, 'I love you."

"He doesn't say that to me anymore.
But underneath what you see is the man I once knew,

and whom I still adore."

I look at my Mum, take a breath and I say,
"Mum, you cannot think that way.
He shouldn't hurt us the way that he does.
Please open your eyes, this is not love."

My mother stares into space and whispers,
"He loves me."
I tell her, "Love does not show bruises and blood.
Love does not put you down.
Love does not kick you while you're down."

My mother realised after a few days,
She and I needed to get away,
That the man she once loved wasn't here anymore.

When my father left to go to the pub,
My mum wrote a note to leave for my Dad:

To the man I once knew,

My Lord, did I love you?
Remember how it used to be?
You were my everything.
Remember when we had our child?
You were such a wonderful father and husband.
Then you started to change,
You became distant after the loss of your job,
You started to lose your love for us,
You became angry and pushed us away,
You lost your job and we were the ones that paid.
You hit us,
You used us, and you abused us,
You took your love away,
That is why I'm leaving you today.

Tell the man I once knew that I loved him,
Tell the man you have become to get help, stop the hurt,
I've finally realised I don't deserve to be treated like dirt.

I stayed for years and I waited around,
For the man I once knew, but he was nowhere to be found.

I took your abuse,

Your anger and your hate,

No more now, you have smashed my last plate,

You have hit us for the last time.

I am no longer yours,

You are no longer mine.

I have to walk away from this with my head held high.

I hope you can change for the better and stay that way.

No one deserves to be treated this way,

that is why we've left and gone away,

Memories will stay, they will forever burn,

Lessons in life are meant to be learned.

I say goodbye and farewell,

Please don't put another woman through hell,

Treat her well,

Change from who you are to all you could be.

Do it for you and do it for me,

The world will thank you so gratefully.

Change,

Rearrange,

Be the better man.

I hope someday you understand why I left,

It was best to get away,

For your soul, I pray,

Change your ways, have better days,

I am off to start anew,

Things will be so different without you.

If only it wasn't like this,

I will give you one final kiss,

I'll say goodbye on this page.

I truly hope you can end your rage.

Start a new book with a fresh page,

Turn over a new leaf,

I know you are reading in disbelief,

I could not keep going, this had to be done.

From someone you once knew,

Please see this from my point of view.
I'll find my setting sun, I've moved on to start a new life,
I hope that you can find yourself a new wife.
But don't treat her the way that you did me,
Find your happiness for all eternity.

I Sit Here

I Sit Here

I sat upon the floor,

Listening to the sounds from behind the closed door,

Listening to the sound of your maniac mind,

You had me in your grasp and you wouldn't let go.

Love was never here,

This is a relationship I have come to fear,

I long for the moment you would hold me near.

Hold me near, my dear,

Stop yelling and fighting,

Don't hold me down like a wolf in the night,

With your endless biting.

You made me give myself to you,

You made me think that it was "love"

I was the glove to your hand.

You work me in ways I don't understand,

You made me be this way,
I'm in constant fear.
When you are good, you're really good to me,
But then in walks a different you, the one I despise.

You say you have an illness,
But you're the Devil in disguise,
You hide behind the words "It's the illness within,"
I have heard that record play before, where do I begin?
Your pathetic lines are the original sin.

You keep me secluded,
I feel so deluded about you.
You painted a picture of everything nice,
A house on the hills, and the picket fences,
Yet here I am putting up defences.

You hit me hard if I "step out of line,"
You always tell me how to dress, how to talk,
I am a living, walking doll,
Everything has to be "just so."

Neatness and order is what you thrashed into me,
Now look at me,
I am a personal robot,
I almost feel emotionless,
I do what you say and pray everything will be okay.

But whatever I do simply isn't good enough,
I may as well die, but if I did, would you cry?
It feels like centuries have come to pass since I have been with you.

I never really see the light of day,
Or feel the sun on my skin.
You keep me within these walls,
To cater to your every whim.
I am nothing more than a toy to you,
My feelings are shattered, they are broken on the floor,
The person I once was doesn't live here anymore.

Love me, you can do it if you try,
But would I really want you?

I can't even stand to look your way,
I hate you within myself for you making me stay.

Oh look, here you come into the room,
What is it you want now?
Do you want to make me pick up a broom?
Do you want me to clean?
Or call me pathetic and act all mean?

I saw that you were dressed in a suit, you began to cry,
I sat looking at you and wondering, is this the same guy?

I just sat there, I couldn't move,
You did not say a word, you just went to sleep,
I sat there not moving, staring in your direction,
I looked in the mirror but could see no reflection.
I knew if I moved you would make me pay,
So, I sat still as the sun went down and sometime later you awoke.

You put your hand on the remote and turned on the TV,

You grabbed yourself a drink of whisky,
Still you were crying,
I tried to make a sound,
But you acted like I wasn't even around.

You cried and you cried and I tried to make a sound,
"Why are you crying?" I asked with fake concern.
Nothing was spoken from your lips,
You took something out of your pocket and put it on the stand.
It was a piece of paper with a picture of me.
"What is this?" I asked,
Again, not a word.
I screamed this time, ***"What is this?"***
Again, you didn't respond,
I screamed and I yelled, I lost all control,
"What is happening?"

I looked at the paper you had placed on the stand,
There was a picture of me, with some words underneath,

"Here lays an angel, who will be missed by all the ones who love her, may she rest in peace."

I started to panic,
I screamed, ***Did I die?***
What happened to me?
My Lord, what did you do to me?
You bastard!
What did you do?

I sat there and I tried to come to terms with what happened to me.
I wondered if I'd live in these walls for eternity.

You said "I am sorry. I didn't mean to treat you like I did. If you could have your life over, things would change. I am so sorry I did this to you."

Hatred began to fill me,
You did this, you must pay,
Why did you take my life away?

I couldn't even remember how,
Moments later it came rushing back to me.

I dare not speak of what happened to me,
To say the unspeakable, details need not be said,
Nothing can change, now I am dead.
I have no idea where I should roam,
Am I stuck here?
I know you aren't sorry,
Guilt is just starting to eat you,
If I was alive, I would try to defeat you.

I never thought those words would need to escape me,
"If I was alive."
I hear a sound coming from the next room,
Something swinging from side to side,
Like a free balloon.
You had hung yourself,
You had caused your own death.

You left behind a letter that said:

I killed her in ways I would never tell.
I killed her slowly for years.
I took her passion, took her pride.
I took a vibrant woman who once was alive.
I do not know if I ever loved her.
I don't think I even know what love really is.

I know I must go now from this place,
Too many memories remain.
I'm leaving and I won't be back again.

After the life left your body,

I saw you standing before me,

You looked up at your swinging body,

You were horrified.

You looked at me with fright in your eyes,

I thought of all the times you must have seen the terror in mine.

You told me you were sorry,

I said to you, "No you're not. You kept me locked up like a prisoner wife, you took away my very life,"

Then from out of each corner of the room,
dark shadows came and took you away,
I looked on as they dragged you down to hell,
I saw terror in your eyes as you were dragged to that tortured place.

I sat there,
I sat there and I wondered where will I end up?
Where will I go?
Will I stay here or will I go?

For years, I remained in the walls,
Life moved on,
New people moved in,
But there I would sit and no one would know.

Still all I seem to do is sit here.

I Need You

I Need You

I needed you to want me and show me the way,
I needed you to love me, I just don't feel that today.
I get ignored, you're bored with me,
You use me and abuse me.

I grew up not knowing love and I thought
You would show me what love was all about,
But now my mind gets flooded with doubt,
I'm always filled with pain,
Here comes the Winter rain,
But it won't wash away the daily strain.

These feelings of mine, they're raw and real,
They're layers of emotions that you can peel,
How I wish I could be strong like steel,
I wish I could control my emotions,
But I am lost, I feel weak,
Salvation is what I forever seek.
I would climb the highest mountain peak,

Just to finally be free.

I don't want to be with you,
And I know you don't want to be with me,
You just want to control everything I do.
I needed you to show me love,
I needed you to show me a different world
To the one I knew before.
You lied to me and cheated on our love.

And now you won't let me go,
Don't make me live this life,
Please say it isn't so.

I once thought I needed you, but I don't anymore,
I don't need this pain; my body is too sore.
There is a world out there for me, I want to explore.

It Needs to End

It Needs to End

Violence needs to end,

We need to be lovers and friends.

We should at least be civil toward one another,

Deep down aren't we all sisters and brothers of this land?

We should walk together, hand in hand,

We should all just rejoice,

We really do have a choice!

Instead, we tear each other down,

We get laughed at and kicked to the ground,

We need others and they aren't around.

Domestic violence is everywhere,

In every country, in every place in the world,

it needs to end; nobody should live in fear.

We need to solve problems,

But not with weapons or fists,

Loved ones shouldn't be hit, they should be kissed.

What in this world have we missed?

Have we lost our way?

Have we forgotten how to care?

When you call out for someone, will they be there?

We need to watch the signs of when domestic violence is taking place, reach out get help,

Seek and you shall find,

Healing can be done over time.

Get some help, seek it out,

You're not the one who is weak,

We will be your voice if you cannot speak.

You're not to blame, it's not your fault.

Too many people seem to think we should blame ourselves, when someone treats us badly,

But the person who treated you madly and badly are the ones we should shame.

They are to blame for the shame they put upon you.

If you speak out and get help, you can be free,

You can get a better life

Away from the abuse and the pain,

You will be sheltered from the rain,

You can start to really live again.

Be free, be you, be me,

Be anything in this world you choose,

Set yourself free from a life of abuse.

Domestic violence, violence of every kind, needs to end.

An Important Message

Domestic abuse is becoming rampant and it needs to be cut out of society like a cancer.

It should never be. So much cruelty and injustice. In the world where people say "trust us", and they are the ones we should never trust.

But if you seek, you shall find the diamonds of the world. Not every person is bad. Not everyone has the madness within. Not everyone will set out to sin. You can win. You *can* be a winner in this world.

You can be *you*. If something is happening that is wrong towards you, then please seek help.

It is **NOT** your fault.

Learn to walk away. People will always play the same old song; "I won't do it again," but they do.

You deserve better in life. Just walk away and play it safe. Reach out to anyone you possibly can. Don't fold towards threatening demands. Please stay strong. You are part of this world and you belong.

Our lives sometimes aren't how we thought they would be, but changes can be made. People can be saved. You can do anything you put your mind to.

Always check in on others. Make sure that everyone is alright. Never take the law into your own hands. Get legal advice and help.

Take care of each other and take care of yourself.

Smile and let light shine on through to your life.

Be safe.
Be happy.
Be you.
Be free.

Feel love.
Feel confident.
Feel special.
Feel free.

Websites providing resources and assistance for Domestic Violence

(Australia)

Our Watch
http://www.ourwatch.org.au/

Luke Batty Foundation
http://lukebattyfoundation.org.au/

White Ribbon
http://www.whiteribbon.org.au/

Domestic Violence Resource Centre
http://www.dvrcv.org.au/support-services/national-services

Domestic Violence Prevention Centre
http://www.domesticviolence.com.au/

Australian Domestic and Family Violence Clearing House
https://www.arts.unsw.edu.au/research/gendered-violence-research-network/

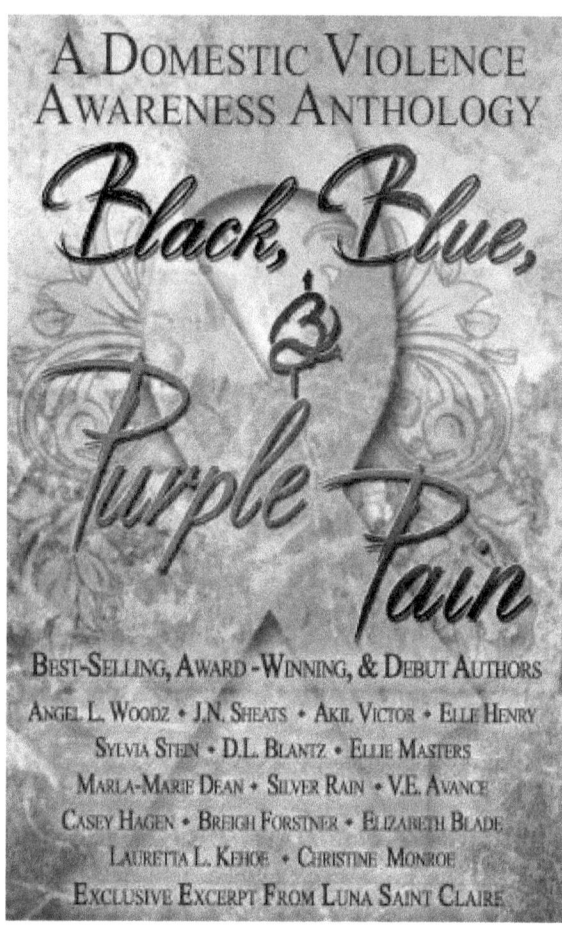

Quotes from the Authors of Black Blue & Purple Pain

Bare Souls by Casey Hagen

"I want to save you from the shadows, Maggie. The little girl she had been, the one who believed in fairy tales, would have prayed for that. I need to save myself."

Website: www.caseyhagenauthor.com

Facebook: https://www.facebook.com/CaseyHagenAuth

Clara's Heart by D.L. Blantz

"I was genuinely loved for once and it felt good—too good."

Facebook: https://www.facebook.com/authordlblantz/

Amazon: amazon.com/author/d.l.blantz

Twitter: https://twitter.com/snowangel200523

The Sleeping Serpent by Luna Saint Claire

"She realized in an instant that being around him awakened her, stirring the sediment that had long ago settled at the bottom of her well. He made her feel a part of him--of something larger, and somehow more alive."

Website: http://www.compelledbooks.com/

Twitter: https://twitter.com/Compelled_Books

Amazon: http://amzn.to/1SKaAGw

Facebook: https://www.facebook.com/CompelledBooks/

MANIPULATED: The Journal of A Bruised Soul by Angel L Woodz

"Just when you thought it was perfect... things aren't always what they seem."

Universal link for the eBook:
https://books2read.com/BlackBluePurplePainAnthology

Facebook: www.facebook.com/LLPromo

Everything Fades Away by Elle Henry

"Tony please don't hurt her!" she begged. Why would she allow him to do this to me? Was he so unhappy with beating her, he needed to take control over me as well? "Please don't hurt me" I cried out from my bruised eyes. The tears stung my face, so I tried not to cry.

Website: www.authorellehenry.com

Twitter: www.twitter.com/candidly_elle

Facebook: www.facebook.com/candidlyellehenry

Instagram: www.instagram.com/tres_chic_editor

Email: Info@authorellehenry.com

Survivor's Block by Akil Victor

"Because they are the perpetrators of the crime, of the violence. Be it verbal or physical. It stems from something and needs to be rooted out. That's why I say to any man, if you have done this before or are capable of doing so, then seek help. Get answers to prevent you from hurting someone on a level of this magnitude. It is said that a woman is beaten every nine seconds in our country. Think about how many lives are altered in those nine seconds. Not just the woman- whom suffers the worst, or the perpetrator who ruins his life in the process, but the witnesses also. The children who are traumatized and will pick-up different views and actions in life as an end result. Everyone loses when domestic violence occurs."

Fairy Circle by Lauretta L. Kehoe

"Maybe it's easier to fight about the little things than to try to deal with what was happening to you. Maybe by fighting about a dress, your mom is trying to assert some independence. Have you ever talked to her about what was happening to you?

Facebook: www.facebook.com/adreamofdragons

Sleepless by J.N. Sheats

"Abusers take. They weasel and worm—manipulating people without a hint of shame or an ounce of regret. Then after every last inch of will is stripped away, they take more...They will always take more, but what else do I have left to give?"

Facebook: https://www.facebook.com/jsheatsart/

Website: www.jnsheats.com

The Devil He Became by Sylvia Stein

November 2013

Dear Diary,

I am not even sure what is happening right now? I look at myself in the mirror and I do not recognize who I am? The spirit which was inside of me once has faded. Each day I am terrified of what the new day is going to bring me.

I am dying inside. Slowly this is not the life I was expecting.

I guess I should have seen this coming.

But Valentin was so kind and gentle and we shared the love of medicine and he was such a good listener and became my best friend.

I thought we would always be happy.

When he proposed, it was so romantic.

I thought nothing could change him. I thought well who knows what I thought.

All I know is everything is suddenly out of control and I am not sure what will happen next.

If only I could go back...

Elizabeth

Website: http://sylviawriter07.wixsite.com/sylvia-author

Facebook: https://www.facebook.com/SylWriter07

Invisible Shackles by Elizabeth Blade

"Every move I make, a step closer you will take, lurking in the corners and darkness of my mind.

I don't want to be yours, you are not mine. But I am confined to this space and time. Let me go, let me be, let these tormented moments be history."

Facebook: https://www.facebook.com/ElizabethBladeWriter

Website: www.elizabethblade.com

Twitter: https://twitter.com/Moondance_81 (@Moondance_81)

Email: moondance_81@me.com

Author's Word

The Author would like to state that violence everywhere whether it is towards a man woman or child needs to stop.

Violence of every kind needs to end. Reach out to a family, friend or someone you can trust.

Men, women and children are subjected to violence,

Enough is enough. Justice must be done. We should rise up together as one.

Let's be a Rising Moon on Domestic Violence and cast the shadows away. Start a brand new day.

Inspiringly Yours,

Elizabeth Blade